I HAVE DYSLEXIA

David P. Hurford, Ph.D.
April Huninghake

Published by JETT Publishing
215 West Adams
Pittsburg, Kansas 66762-5133

Copyright © 2015 by JETT Publishing. All rights reserved. No part of this book may be reproduced in any form, electronic or mechanical, including photocopy, recording, or any information storage and retrieval system, without permission in writing from the publisher.

ISBN: 978-1-63452-857-3

www.JETTPublishing.net

This book is dedicated to all of the boys, girls and adults who have dyslexia; to reading scientists who are helping us understand dyslexia; to the parents and advocates who are working to bring the science to the practitioners; and to the teachers and dyslexia specialists who are using this information to help individuals with dyslexia become competent readers.

You are probably reading this book because you have a difficult time reading. You might be reading this book with your mom or dad because you need help reading.

This book was written for you!

The first thing that you need to know...

... is that you are not alone! Many people have a difficult time learning to read. In your classroom, there are probably four or five other students who are finding reading to be very difficult. In a class of 20 students, about four will struggle with reading.

There are even adults who have difficulty reading.

Here are some adults you may have heard of who had difficulty learning to read just like you:

- Dr. Helen Taussig (founded the field of pediatric cardiology)
- Steven Spielberg (movie director, writer, & producer)
- Bella Thorne (actress, singer, model, & dancer)
- Henry Winkler (actor – "The Fonz")
- Jennifer Aniston (actress)
- Jack Horner (paleontologist; advisor to *Jurassic Park* & others)
- Cher (singer & actress)
- Dav Pilkey (author of *Captain Underpants*)

JACK HORNER

When people have a very difficult time learning to read they might have dyslexia.

The word dyslexia means "difficult word."
 - "Dys" means difficult and "lexis" means word.

Dyslexia means to have a difficulty reading words.

When we are born, we have the ability to speak any language. Babies just have to hear the language and they will eventually start speaking it.

It is natural for babies to learn to speak. If a baby is born in China and then brought up in the United States by people who speak English, the baby will eventually speak English.

If a baby is born in the United States and then brought up in France by people who speak French, the baby will eventually speak French.

It takes a while for children to speak well, but they do it naturally.

Unfortunately, we are not born with the ability to know how to read. It takes a LOT of practice. Even for most people who do not have dyslexia, it takes a long time to be a good reader.

It is even more difficult to learn to read English than it is to learn to read other languages!

This is because the writing system used in the English language is very confusing.

The key to learning to read is that we have to learn that different letters represent different sounds. For example, the letter "F" represents the /f/ sound. The letters are actually a "code." We use this code to read by translating or "decoding" the letters into sounds and then combining those sounds into words. We also use the code to write. We think of the sounds that are in a word and then write the letters that represent those sounds.

For people who have dyslexia, learning the code is very, very, very difficult. You might ask why it would be so difficult to learn the code? The answer is that it has to do with our brains. Everyone's brain is a little different.

That is a very good thing.

You have some friends who are better at drawing. You also have some friends who are better at running or throwing, or catching, or music, or math, or thinking up good stories.

We all have things we are really good at doing.

It is also a good thing that we are not all good at the same things. We need people to be better at different things so that some people will be good at designing roads and others will be good at building them. Some people will be good at discovering things and others will be good at figuring out ways to use them.

We all have different abilities and that is a great thing!

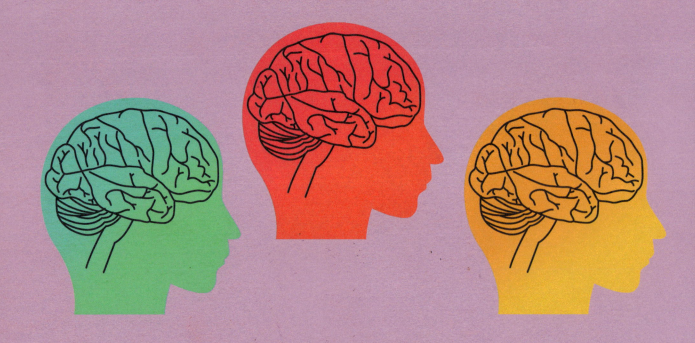

The reason that we are really good at doing those different things is because our brains are different.

For the most part, our brains are like other people's brains, but the way our brains are connected on the inside is often a little bit different than other people's.

Remember, that is a good thing.

When you see a picture of a brain, it might not look very interesting to you. On the inside of our brains are different parts. These parts do different things. Some parts allow us to hear, other parts allow us to see, to think, to run.

We cannot do anything without our brains!

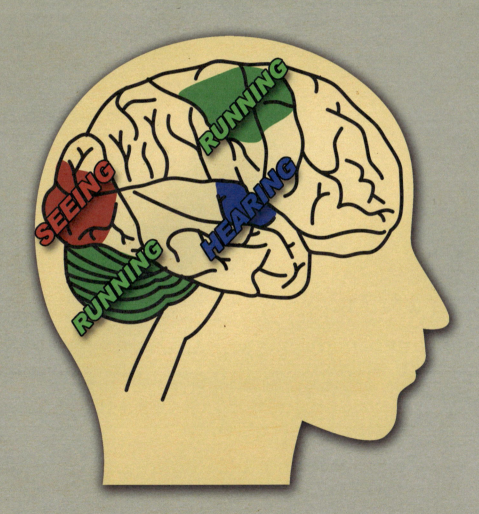

Other parts of the brain are used to get information from one part of the brain to another part of the brain. These parts are like roads or highways. They help to move information from one part to another part.

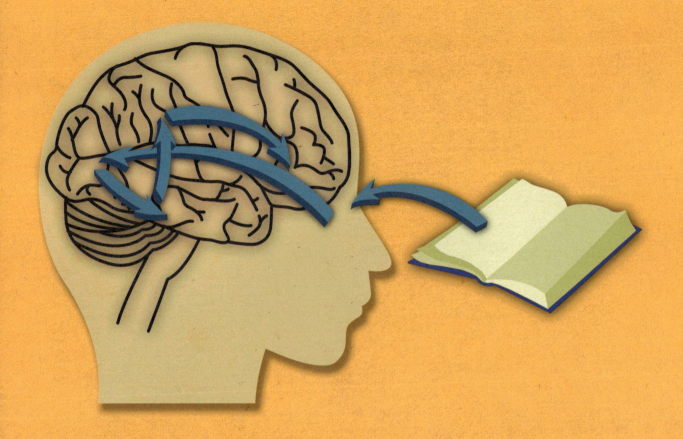

When a person reads they have to see what they are reading. That information is sent from our eyes to the part of the brain that allows us to see the letters. That part of the brain is in the back. That information is then sent to a different part of the brain that has information stored in it about the sounds of the letters.

Then that information is sent to another different part of the brain that deals with information about language.

The brain works with all of that information just like a computer. For people who have brains that have all of those areas and all of the connections between them working together, they can learn to read. For people who have dyslexia, some of those areas are not very strong. The connections between those areas are not very strong either.

So, it is very difficult to learn to read.

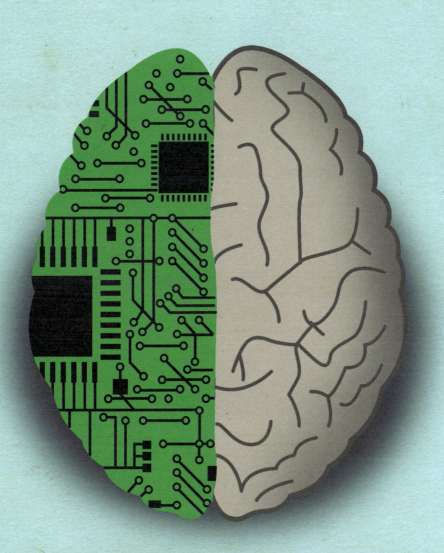

The good news is that reading scientists have discovered that we can strengthen those areas and connections.

People who have dyslexia can learn to read! They may not be the fastest readers in the world, but they will be able to read. As it turns out, being a fast reader is not that important. What is important is being able to read and being able to understand what you are reading.

Strengthening those areas and connections of the brain is challenging, but you can do it! It is going to take a lot of work and practice, but you can become a good reader.

So, let's get started!

All of the profits from sales of this book are donated to the Center for the Assessment and Remediation of Reading Difficulties.

CARRD, Inc. is a nonprofit organization dedicated to assisting individuals with dyslexia and reading disabilities to become competent readers.

www.CARRDInc.org

Dyslexia Risk Calculator

Questions (Circle the appropriate number)	YES	NO
1. Does your child avoid reading?	2	0
2. When reading a word, does your child sound out the first letter or two of the word and guess the rest of the sounds of the word?	3	0
3. Does your child know all of the names of the letters of the alphabet?	0	2
4. Does your child know the sounds that each letter represents?	0	2
5. Does your child reverse letters when spelling?	2	0
6. Is your child's teacher concerned about your child's reading ability?	2	0
7. Does your child have poor handwriting?	1	0
8. Does your child have a difficult time comprehending what he or she is reading?	3	0
9. Does your child easily forget what he or she just read?	3	0
10. Has your child's teacher told you that your child is reading below grade level?	2	0
To Score: Add all of the numbers that are circled.	Total:	

If the total is larger than 8, your child may be at risk for reading difficulties. To get a better understanding of your child's potential risk for dyslexia, please visit www.ReadingScreening.org.

For more information regarding dyslexia, please visit:

CARRD, Inc.
www.CARRDInc.org

The Center for Research Evaluation & Awareness of Dyslexia
www.pittstate.edu/READing

The International Dyslexia Association
www.eida.org

Decoding Dyslexia
www.DecodingDyslexia.net

About the Illustrator and Author

David P. Hurford, Ph.D. is a professor of psychology and counseling at Pittsburg State University. He directs the Center for Research, Evaluation and Awareness of Dyslexia (Center for READing) and is the founder and manager of the Center for the Assessment and Remediation of Reading Difficulties (CARRD, Inc.), a nonprofit organization dedicated to assisting individuals with dyslexia become competent readers. He earned his doctorate in developmental psychology from the University of Akron, an M.A. from Hollins University and an A.B. from Drury University. He has published articles in the area of dyslexia, reading difficulties, phonological processing and other educational issues. Early in his career, he was the recipient of a Spencer Fellowship from the National Academy of Education, which allowed him to dedicate his efforts toward the prevention, identification and intervention of dyslexia and reading difficulties. More recently, he has authored a reading curriculum designed to prevent reading difficulties in kindergarten (Secret Codes) and first grade (Advanced Codes). He loves to help individuals with dyslexia and reading difficulties to become competent readers.

April Huninghake is a graphic designer, illustrator, and photographer with a B.F.A. in illustration and a B.S.T. in graphic design. She manages a local screen print shop, works for the Pittsburg State University Theatre, and takes on other freelance art and design when she can. Her styles range from fully digital creations to mixed media to fully traditional works of art. From a young age she has helped to care for children and hopes to use her art and design skills to produce imagery that will positively impact children's lives.

Made in United States
Troutdale, OR
03/01/2024